RHS
Inspiring everyone to grow

Let's Get Gardening

DK

DK | Penguin Random House

Senior editor **Satu Hämeenaho-Fox**
Designer **Rachael Hare**
Design assistants **Eleanor Bates, Kitty Glavin**
Art editors **Seepiya Sahni, Jaileen Kaur**
Senior art editor **Nidhi Mehra**
Editor **Radhika Haswani**
Picture researcher **Sakshi Saluja**
Pre-production producer **Dragana Puvacic**
Producer **John Casey**
Jacket designer **Rachael Hare**
Jacket co-ordinator **Isobel Walsh**
Managing editor **Penny Smith**
Managing art editor **Mabel Chan**
Creative director **Helen Senior**
Publishing director **Sarah Larter**

RHS publisher **Rae Spencer-Jones**
RHS consultant **Simon Maughan**

First published in Great Britain in 2019 by
Dorling Kindersley Limited in association
with the Royal Horticultural Society.
80 Strand, London, WC2R 0RL.

Copyright © 2019 Dorling Kindersley Limited
A Penguin Random House Company
10 9 8 7 6 5 4 3 2 1
001–314398–May/2019

A CIP catalogue record for this book
is available from the British Library.
ISBN: 978-0-2413-8263-9

Printed in China

A WORLD OF IDEAS:
SEE ALL THERE IS TO KNOW

www.dk.com

This book contains content previously
published in DK and RHS titles *How Does
My Garden Grow?*; *Ready, Steady, Grow*;
Grow It, Eat It; and *Wildlife Gardening*.

Contents

Be an eco-friendly gardener

Being eco-friendly means thinking about how what we do affects nature, from tiny seedlings to huge trees, and the animals that rely on them. It's also about keeping in mind that you are part of nature too. Get out there and get gardening!

What does an eco-friendly gardener do?

Grows vegetables
Vegetables that you've grown yourself are by far the best. They are healthy to eat, save money, and help the environment by reducing pollution from the vehicles that carry them to supermarkets. No plastic packaging here!

Protects wildlife
We can attract wildlife to our gardens by planting plants that encourage animals to visit, and giving them a safe home. Gardens are a vital habitat for animals in cities where many areas have been paved over.

Reduces waste

We can re-use and recycle things from the home so we don't have to throw them away. Food waste can be used as compost, while broken items can find a new use in the garden.

Makes home greener

Bring plants inside to help make your home prettier and healthier. Plants clean the air and make for a much nicer indoor environment.

Gets healthy

Gardening is good for you! Research has shown that digging in soil makes you feel happier, and it's also good exercise.

What is a plant?

A plant is a living thing that makes food from sunlight. There are nearly 400,000 types of plant! They have flowers, leaves, stems, and roots.

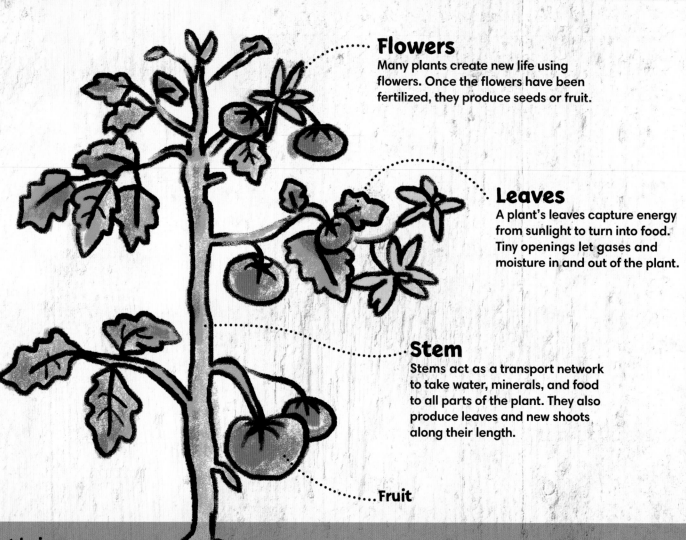

Flowers
Many plants create new life using flowers. Once the flowers have been fertilized, they produce seeds or fruit.

Leaves
A plant's leaves capture energy from sunlight to turn into food. Tiny openings let gases and moisture in and out of the plant.

Stem
Stems act as a transport network to take water, minerals, and food to all parts of the plant. They also produce leaves and new shoots along their length.

Fruit

Root hairs
These take up water from the soil.

Roots
Roots suck up the water and nutrients from the soil that the plant needs to grow.

Root tip
This part grows into the soil.

How do plants grow?

Seed leaf

True leaf

Seeds contain everything a new plant needs to grow: the baby plant itself and food to get it started.

When the conditions are right, the seed takes in water, swells, and splits its case. The main root reaches down into the soil.

One or two tiny seed leaves shoot out, quickly followed by the first true leaves. The seedling can now make its own food.

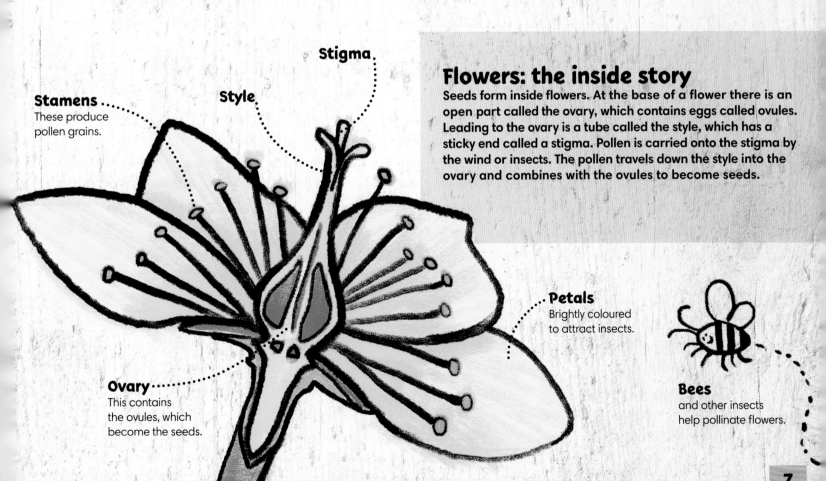

Stigma

Style

Stamens
These produce pollen grains.

Flowers: the inside story

Seeds form inside flowers. At the base of a flower there is an open part called the ovary, which contains eggs called ovules. Leading to the ovary is a tube called the style, which has a sticky end called a stigma. Pollen is carried onto the stigma by the wind or insects. The pollen travels down the style into the ovary and combines with the ovules to become seeds.

Petals
Brightly coloured to attract insects.

Ovary
This contains the ovules, which become the seeds.

Bees
and other insects help pollinate flowers.

7

What Plants need

Plants adapt to their environments — some like hot, dry weather, some like lots of rain, while others like sandy soil. Whenever you buy a plant from a garden centre, or grow one from seed, make sure you give it what it needs to thrive.

Check the labels

Read labels and seed packets when you buy plants and seeds. These tell you:

- What the plant will look like
- When to sow
- How to sow
- When to plant out in the garden
- When to harvest
- If the plant likes sun or shade
- The type of soil it prefers

These tomatoes have grape-sized fruit in bunches, ideal for hanging baskets.

● Sow   ● Plant out   ○ Harvest

Spring	Summer	Autumn	Winter

Sowing and growing

- Sow indoors in early spring
- Sow seeds 6 mm (¼ in) deep in free-draining seed compost
- Plant outdoors in late spring or early summer
- Harvest late summer to autumn
- Likes full sun
- Prefers warm, well-drained soil

The front of the seed packet shows the variety of the plant and what it will look like when fully grown.

Soil

This is vital to plants. It anchors their roots and acts as a store of water and nutrients. Not all soils are the same, so gardeners often add compost made from dead plant material (like you'd find on a compost heap) to their soil to improve it.

Seed compost

A fine-textured mix that holds water well. It is low in nutrients because seeds already have their own store of food.

General-purpose compost

An all-round compost mixture that looks like soil. Most plants in this book will grow well in general-purpose compost.

Grow-bag compost

This is a nutrient-rich mixture specially prepared for hungry vegetables, such as peppers.

Sunlight

Like people, plants need energy to grow and reproduce. But unlike people, plants make their own food through a process called photosynthesis. To do this, plants take in carbon dioxide gas (CO_2) from the air and water from the soil, then use sunlight to convert them into glucose (a type of sugar). The plants then release waste oxygen gas (O_2) into the air.

> **Carbon dioxide + water + sunlight = glucose + oxygen**

O_2

CO_2

Water

Water

Without water, plants wilt and die. However, most plants don't like waterlogged roots, so make holes in the bottom of the container and add broken pot or small stones to help the water drain. Always water plants before and after you plant them in a new pot.

Broken pot

Peat-based compost
Carnivorous (meat-eating) plants, such as sundews, need peat-based compost. Sometimes coir (coconut) fibre is used instead of peat.

Aquatic soil
This contains a slow-release fertilizer that does not leak into water. This helps prevent algae and weeds growing in the pond. Ordinary garden soil can also be used.

Mulch
Mulches are used to cover soil and help keep it moist. They also stop weeds growing. Typical mulches include small stones, shells, straw, or wood chips.

Gardening tools

You don't need many special tools to get gardening. As long as you have soil, seeds, and water you'll be able to grow things. Gardening tools such as a spade and fork will make bigger jobs such as digging holes a lot easier.

For gardening outdoors

Fork
For breaking up the soil so plants can spread their roots

Spade
For digging holes in the soil

Plant pots
Collect pots of varying sizes for different plants

Trowel
For filling pots and covering seeds with soil

Watering can
For watering indoor and outdoor plants

Gardening gloves
Thick gloves for dealing with rough or spiky plants

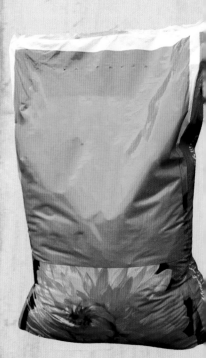

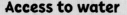

Access to water
All plants need water to grow

Liquid feed
Food for plants that need extra nutrients

Compost
Rich compost gives plants a better chance to grow than ordinary soil

Plastic bottle
Useful for various gardening projects

Spray bottle
For spritzing delicate plants such as ferns

Pot and tray
To grow plants in, and catch water that drains out

Glass jar
For storage and craft projects

Soil
For planting your seeds and plants in

Gravel
Makes your plant projects look neater and deters slugs

Tools for making things

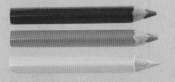

Colour pencils
For decorating labels and creating papercrafts

Scissors
Ask for a grown-up's help with sharp scissors

Pens
Write your labels using permanent marker

Modelling clay
Useful for sticking your labels in so they stand up

Tape
Useful for sticking things down or creating guides for drawing

Lolly sticks
Use these to label your seeds so you know what is in the pot

Kitchen garden

Fruit, vegetables, and herbs taste best when they are home-grown. Learn how with these tasty activities.

13

What is a kitchen garden?

A kitchen garden is anywhere you grow things to eat. It can be any size, from a small collection of containers to a large raised bed.

Vegetable patch

If you've got a large space in your garden, you can sow all sorts of things. The plants shown here are happy in most types of soil and can be planted in pots or in the ground outside.

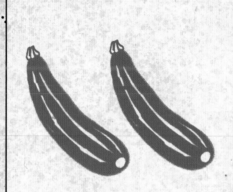

Courgettes

Carrots

Beetroot

Sweetcorn

Windowsill

Herbs and other plants that love a warm, sunny spot will be happy all year round on a windowsill. You can also grow seedlings to plant outdoors in the spring.

Blueberries

Canes

Narrow spaces work well for plants that like to climb. Berries such as raspberries can be grown up canes.

Trees

If you have the space, a fruit tree will provide things to eat year after year. How about an apple, pear, plum, or cherry tree?

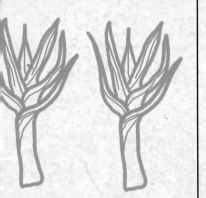

Leeks

Onions

Pumpkins

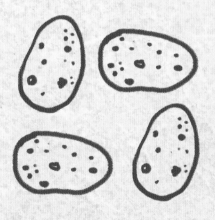

Potatoes

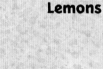

Strawberries

Lemons

Pots and containers

Many plants like to get started in a container. You can grow your plants to a good size and then plant them outside in the soil. You can also leave them in their containers – it makes them much easier to move about!

Raised beds

A raised bed is a box made of wooden planks. You can fill it with any type of soil, so choose one that best suits the plants you want to grow.

Lettuce

Growing herbs

Herbs such as oregano, parsley, and thyme can be easily grown from seed. However, in winter it's best to grow them on a sunny windowsill from ready-grown herbs in pots.

Herbs like to be in a warm, sunny place outdoors. A bit of shade is okay but don't put them somewhere that is always shady.

You will need

Cartons

Scissors

Pen or pencil

Large paper clips

Stones

General-purpose compost

Paper or card

Herb seeds

1

Collect a number of fruit juice cartons. These will make colourful containers for your herbs. They also have a waterproof lining and will not fall apart.

2

Cut off the top quarter of the carton using scissors. Then make drainage holes in the bottom using a pen or pencil.

3

Join your containers together with large paper clips. Arrange them in a pattern – they look better if you put any writing to the back.

4

Put a few stones at the bottom of each carton for drainage, then fill them with general-purpose compost. It may be easier to do this if you make a cone out of paper or card.

5

Sprinkle a few oregano, parsley, and thyme seeds into separate cartons. Cover with a thin layer of compost, water, and leave in a well-lit place to germinate. Keep the herbs lightly watered.

6

Pull out some of the seedlings if they get crowded. You can eat the little plants you've pulled out. Don't let your herbs dry out.

How to Grow
Carrots

You can grow all kinds of carrots – large ones, round ones, and different coloured ones. The first wild carrots were purple, yellow, or white and tasted bitter but, over the centuries, gardeners have bred all colours of carrot to be sweet and juicy.

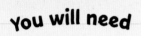

You will need

Hessian bag

Bin liner

Stapler

Carrot seeds

Sand

Compost

Liquid fertilizer

You can keep carrots for months after you've dug them up. Trim off the leaves, then layer them in slightly damp sand, making sure they aren't touching.

1

Line a hessian bag with a bin liner, stapled in place. Poke a few drainage holes in the bottom of the bag.

2

Carrot seeds are small so you might want to mix them with a little sand so you can plant them evenly.

3

Fill your container with compost. Make shallow trenches. Thinly sprinkle the seeds in the trenches and cover them with more compost.

4

Thin out your carrots as they push through the soil by pulling out about half of the plants. Leave a gap of roughly 5 cm (2 in) between them.

5

Carrots need plenty of water as they grow. Add a general-purpose liquid fertilizer once a week when the leaves start to grow rapidly.

6

When the carrots are big enough to eat (around 12 weeks after planting) lift them from the compost. Give them a wash before eating them!

How to Grow Potatoes

Potatoes are easy and fun to grow. Everybody loves eating them – as golden roasties, creamy mash, fabulous fries, and crunchy crisps.

You will need

Seed potatoes

Egg box

Hessian sack

Bin liner

Compost

Scissors

Don't plant more than four or five seed potatoes in your sack.

1

Put seed potatoes, with their sprouting "eyes" pointing up, in an empty egg box. Leave them in a light, unheated place until they sprout.

2

Line a rolled-down hessian sack with a bin liner. Make drainage holes in the bottom. Cover the potatoes in general-purpose compost, with the shoots pointing up.

3

When leaves grow, cover the stalks with compost and partly roll up the sack. This is called earthing up. More potatoes will grow off the stalks.

4

Keep earthing up as the plants grow. Unroll the bag and sack a little each time until it is fully unrolled.

5

The potatoes are ready for harvesting when the leaves begin to turn yellow. Cut the sack to get them out.

6

Remove the potatoes and leave them on the soil for a few hours to dry out.

How to Grow
Beetroot

There are white and yellow varieties of beetroot but the most well-known colour is a deep purple-red. Beetroot is yummy in salads or pickled in vinegar.

You will need

- Container
- Beetroot seeds
- Soil
- Fork

Don't put the plants too close together. The roots need space to grow.

1 Make holes 2.5 cm (1 in) deep in a large container. Sow two seeds into each hole, cover with soil, and water.

2 Thin the seedlings when they are 2.5 cm (1 in) high, by taking out one of the seedlings from each hole.

3 Keep the plants well watered. Dry spells can cause the beetroots to become woody and split.

4 Pick when each beetroot is the size of a ping-pong ball. Lift the beetroot and use a fork to lever under the root.

Beetroot leaves can be eaten like spinach. Twist off the tops with your hands, rather than cutting with a knife.

How to Grow
Lettuce

Flat or curly, green or purple, there are many varieties of crispy lettuce leaves. Sow the seeds at any time through the spring and summer.

1 In a pot of seed compost, use a pencil to make a hole 1.5 cm (½ in) deep.

2 Take a pinch of lettuce seeds and sprinkle them in each hole in your pot.

You will need

- Plant pots
- Seed compost
- Pencil
- Lettuce seeds
- Label
- Gravel

3 Using your fingertips, cover the seeds with compost then water. Label with the variety of lettuce.

4 Once the seedlings start to grow, pull some out to allow space for good growth.

5 Once they have grown to this size, plant each lettuce into its own pot. Pour gravel around the base to deter hungry slugs.

Try growing crops in a wooden crate. Line it with a bin bag and fill with compost, then sow the seeds. The wood keeps in valuable warmth and moisture.

6

7

Water often to keep the soil moist. This needs to be done once or twice a day in warm weather.

Pick the outer leaves when you need them. Your lettuce will keep growing more leaves.

How to Grow Leeks

Grown for more than 6,000 years, leeks are thought to have been eaten by the ancient Egyptians! Now you can grow these ancient vegetables too.

Leeks hate competing with weeds, so make sure you keep the soil around them free of wild plants.

You will need

- Small and large pots
- Soil
- Leek seeds
- Scissors
- Liquid feed
- Trowel

1

Fill pots with soil. Make a hole 1.5 cm (½ in) deep with your finger or a pencil, and put in a few leek seeds. Cover with soil, and water. You can keep your pots outdoors.

2

Once the seedlings are growing healthily, water them well. Then make some holes 15 cm (6 in) deep in a large pot. Now lift out the seedlings and carefully separate them.

3

Trim each leek's root ends to 2.5 cm (1 in) long with scissors. Then place each one into its own hole in the large pot.

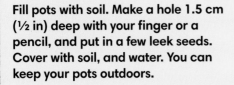

4

Fill each hole with water. The soil washed in will hold each leek in place. Continue to water regularly and use a liquid feed once a month.

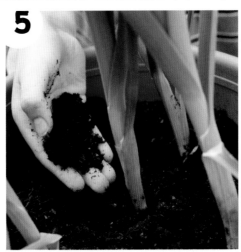

5

Get longer leeks by adding more soil to the pot, raising the soil level around the base of each leek.

6

Lift some baby leeks when small. You can leave other leeks in for longer – even over winter – to grow bigger.

How to Grow Spinach

All parts of spinach plants have been cooked or used in medicines since ancient times. The tasty leaves and stalks help to keep us healthy and strong.

You will need

- Long container
- Compost
- Ruler
- Spinach seeds
- Liquid feed
- Fertilizer
- Scissors

1 Make a trench 2.5 cm (1 in) deep, using a ruler. Sow spinach seeds thinly along the row from mid-spring.

2 Once germinated, thin the seedlings to 8 cm (3 in) apart. Thin them again at a later stage if necessary.

3 Keep well watered, use a liquid feed once a month, and add a nitrogen-rich fertilizer to the soil.

4 Cut off flowering shoots. This will help the plant to produce better leaves.

5 Encourage new growth by picking a few leaves when they get longer than 5 cm (2 in).

Grow spinach in
a cool place, out
of direct sunlight.

How to Grow Chillies

Spicy chilli peppers make curries and noodles taste delicious. They grow well in very warm spots with lots of sunlight. Grow them in the summer for the best results.

You will need

- Chilli seeds
- Seed starting pots
- Soil
- Medium pots
- Fertilizer

Cut the chilli fruit off the plant rather than pulling. If the plant is outside, do this before the end of summer!

1 Sprinkle the seeds in starting pots full of soil. Cover the seeds with a thin layer of soil and keep them warm.

2 Once the seeds poke up through the soil (7 to 10 days after sowing), water them every couple of days.

3 When the plants are big enough, carefully move them into medium-sized pots.

4 Put your plants in a sunny spot. Water every few days. Once fruit starts to appear, give them tomato feed once a week.

Wash your hands after touching chillies as they could sting your eyes.

How to Grow Aubergines

Aubergines evolved from a spiny plant from India with a small, white egg-shaped fruit. This is why an aubergine is also known as an eggplant.

You will need

- Yoghurt pot
- Trowel
- Seed compost
- Aubergine seeds
- Label
- Container
- Spray bottle
- Liquid feed
- Cane
- String

1

Make holes in the base of a clean yoghurt pot and fill with seed compost. Make a hole about 6 mm (¼ in) deep in the compost.

2

Sow two seeds in the hole and brush soil over them with your fingers. Add a label, water, and keep on a windowsill.

3

After the plants start sprouting, remove the smaller seedling to allow the other one more space to continue growing.

4

When spring comes, tip the plant out and place into a hole in a large container of soil. Pat the soil around it and water.

5

Water little but often. If you have a greenhouse, your plant will flourish there.

6

Aubergine flowers are colourful to attract insects for pollinating. Pollination allows the flowers to turn into aubergines.

7

Spray the fruits that develop from the flowers with water. As the fruits start to swell, add liquid feed.

8

Once your plant grows to 30 cm (12 in) tall, pinch or snip off the growing stems at the top. This encourages the rest of the plant to grow. Tie your plant to a cane for support.

9

Pick each fruit when it is 10 cm (4 in) long and has a shine on its skin. You might get between five and ten fruits over a few months.

How to Grow Courgettes

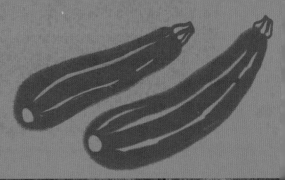

Courgettes are vegetables that can be many odd shapes, colours, and sizes. Why not grow a different variety each year?

1

Push two seeds on their sides into a 1.5 cm (½ in) deep hole in a pot of soil. Water, label, and place on a windowsill.

2

Once the plants start to sprout, remove the weakest seedling and put the other outside. Protect it with part of a plastic bottle.

You will need

- Courgette seeds
- Plant pot
- Soil
- Label
- Plastic bottle
- Liquid feed
- Knife

3

When the roots begin to show through the bottom of the pot, tip the young plant out of its pot, supporting its stem.

4

Place the plant in a hole in a flowerbed, pat soil around it, and water.

5

The bright yellow flowers attract insects, which pollinate the flowers so they can become fruit.

Courgettes are young marrows. You can leave a few attached to turn into mighty marrows, which can grow twice as long.

6 Water the soil around the plant rather than straight onto it, as this could cause it to rot. Give it some liquid plant feed.

7 Pick the flower from the tip of the growing courgette. These can be cooked and eaten.

8 Cut the courgettes at their base when they reach 10 cm (4 in). Ask an adult to help you with the knife.

How to Grow Pumpkins

These large, heavy fruits belong to the squash family. Although some squashes grow quickly, pumpkins can take a long time to ripen.

You will need

Plant pot

Soil

Pumpkin seed

Large container

Canes

String

Plant food

Netting

Mulch

Knife

Pumpkins are one of nature's biggest vegetables. Record-breaking pumpkins can weigh more than 450 kg (1,000 lbs)!

1

In spring, make a 1.5 cm (½ in) deep hole in a pot of soil. Sow one seed on its side, cover with soil, water, and put on a windowsill.

2

Keep well watered. Your plant is ready to transplant once the roots poke out of the bottom of the pot.

3

Make a hole in a large container of soil. Carefully place the plant into the hole. Pat soil around it and water.

4

Wrap and tie the stem around four canes. As the stem grows, keep wrapping and tying it to the canes.

5

Keep the soil well watered. Your plant will produce flowers, attracting insects to pollinate.

6

Feed your plant with plant food every few weeks once the fruits start to form.

7

Make a net hammock to support fruit growing above the ground. Attach the hammock to two of the canes.

8

Add mulch around fruit growing on the ground. Keep turning the fruit slightly to ripen evenly.

9

Cut the fruit off once it has fully matured. Ask an adult to help you cut it and lift it.

How to Grow Beans

Runner beans or french beans, green beans or dwarf beans, you'll have a tough choice deciding which beans to grow!

1 Push four canes into a large pot of soil and tie them together at the top.

2 Plant the beans 5 cm (2 in) deep on each side of a cane. Cover with soil, water, and label.

You will need

- Canes
- Plant pot
- Soil
- Beans
- Label
- Straw or mulch
- Liquid feed

3 Wind each seedling around a cane. It will grow up it. Cover the soil with straw or mulch.

4 Squirt off any aphids (small green insects) with water. Keep watering the soil often and use a liquid feed every two weeks.

5 Pick the bean pods when they are long but still tender. Pick often so that new beans will grow.

Since ancient times, beans have been eaten as a good source of protein.

How to Grow Peppers

Next time you buy peppers, don't throw away the seeds, but plant them instead. Choose fresh orange or red peppers for your seeds, as these are most likely to grow.

1 Cut open your pepper, then use the handle of a spoon to gently push out the seeds.

2 Wash the seeds in water to get rid of a natural anti-germinating substance that stops the seeds growing inside the fruit.

You will need

- Ripe pepper
- Knife
- Spoon
- Pots
- Seed compost
- Grow-bag compost
- Tomato fertilizer
- Mulch

3 Plant your seeds about 6 mm (¼ in) deep in pots filled with seed compost.

4 When the plants fill their pots, plant them in large containers of grow-bag compost. Feed with tomato fertilizer every two weeks.

5 Water regularly. To keep the compost damp, cover it with mulch as this helps hold in the moisture.

Plant watch

The peppers you grow may not look the same as your original pepper! Many supermarket peppers are hybrids (plants whose parents were different varieties), so their offspring may take after one of the parents.

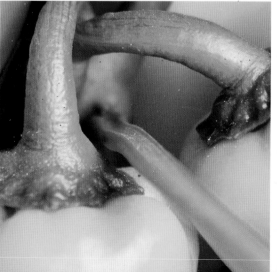

How to grow Sweetcorn

If you grow your own sweetcorn, you can pick it and cook it, or eat it straight off the plant. This is when it is sweetest. You can also grow corn to make popcorn.

1

Sweetcorn is a kind of maize. Its seeds are the dried kernels of corn on the cob.

2

Sow the seeds about 1.5 cm (½ in) deep in compost. Water regularly and keep in a warm place until the seeds start to sprout.

You will need

- Dried kernel seeds
- Compost
- Containers
- Cardboard
- Grow-bag compost
- Tomato fertilizer
- Canes

3

Once the leaves appear, start putting your plants outside in the sun for a few hours each day.

4

Sweetcorn has long roots, so choose a large container. Cover any holes with cardboard or plastic bags with drainage holes.

5

Plant in grow-bag compost, without disturbing the roots. Stand your plants in full sunlight and keep them well watered.

Sweetcorn is pollinated by the wind. The female flowers are the "silks", the long parts that hang out of the ear of corn to catch pollen blown by the wind from another plant. Each pollinated silk becomes one kernel of corn.

6

If roots appear on the surface, cover them over with compost. Feed with tomato fertilizer every two weeks.

7

Support your plants on canes as they grow. The cobs are ready to test when the silks turn brown.

How to Grow Tomatoes

Even when you are short of space, you can still grow an impressive pot of little tomatoes. The tomatoes shown here are a type called "100s and 1000s", but there are lots of varieties to choose from.

You will need

Containers

Seed compost

Seeds

Hammer and nail

Tape

General-purpose compost

When tiny fruits begin to appear, feed the plants with tomato food to help them ripen.

1

Fill a pot with seed compost. Sprinkle seeds onto the compost and cover with 6 mm (¼ in) more compost.

2

Keep the seeds in a warm place. When the seedlings start to grow, move to a sunny position.

3

Ask an adult to make drainage holes in a large container with a hammer, nail, and tape to stop the nail slipping.

4

Transplant two or three plants into general-purpose compost, without disturbing the roots.

5

Firm the compost around the plants, making sure all the roots are covered.

6

Put the plants back in their sunny spot and keep them well watered as they grow.

How to Grow Blueberries

Blueberry bushes grow well in pots filled with acidic (or "ericaceous") soil. Care for them year after year and you'll be rewarded with loads of fruit.

You will need

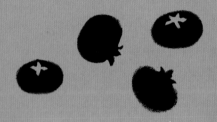

- Large pot
- Compost
- Blueberry plant
- Mulch
- Netting
- Rainwater

Blueberry bushes grow best in a mixture of ericaceous compost and peat.

1

Fill your pot with compost and carefully drop in your blueberry plant. Press down more compost around the plant.

2

Mulch around the new plant using bark or pine needles, which are fairly acidic. Do this again each spring.

3

If your new plant already has some berries, cover it with netting to stop birds from eating the berries.

4

Water the new plant well from spring to autumn using rainwater (tap water will make the soil less acidic).

Blueberries form in clusters, but ripen at different times. Pick each berry a few days after it turns a deep blue colour.

How to Grow Strawberries

Follow the steps below and you will have delicious red strawberries to enjoy eating in the summer, year after year.

1 Start off with a strawberry plug. The neat root ball makes the plug easy to plant and quick to grow.

2 Place the plug in a medium pot of soil. The top of the roots should be level with the soil. Water well.

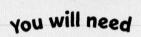

You will need

- Strawberry plug
- Medium pot
- Soil
- Straw
- Feed

There are about 200 seeds on the outer skin of each strawberry.

3 Put straw under the plant to stop the strawberries lying on the ground.

4 Water every day. Once the plant starts flowering, give it liquid feed every 10 days.

5 Check to see if any strawberries have turned red. As soon as one is ripe, pick straight away. Water often as the strawberries begin to swell.

Cover your plant with netting if birds are eating the strawberries.

How to Grow Lemons

A lemon tree needs year-round care to grow lots of lemons. Cover your tree in winter and feed it every month from early spring to late summer.

You will need

- Lemon seeds or young lemon tree
- Pots
- Trowel
- Citrus compost
- Mulch

Growing from seed

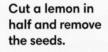

Lemon seed

Cut a lemon in half and remove the seeds.

Select the undamaged seeds. Sow them while they are still moist.

Have patience! It's likely to take many years before your fruit grows.

Growing from a young tree

1 Choose a lemon tree that is ready to begin fruiting. Place it upright in a pot filled with citrus compost.

2 Add 5 cm (2 in) mulch around the trunk to keep in moisture and water often to begin with.

3 As the tree grows, water only when the topsoil looks dry. During the winter, the tree will need less watering.

Lemons contain the most vitamin C of any citrus fruit. In the past, sailors ate them on voyages to stay healthy.

Wildlife garden

Learn how to create wild spaces where garden creatures can live, eat, and grow.

Why be a wildlife gardener?

It is so exciting to see animals flourish in a beautiful garden YOU created. Creatures will visit your garden with only a little encouragement and they work hard to keep your garden healthy.

Pest control

Lots of creatures can damage your garden, but by providing a home for a variety of wildlife you can create a natural balance. Ladybirds love to eat aphids, spiders catch mosquitoes in their webs, and blue tits devour caterpillars.

Flower power

Bees and butterflies are pollinators. This means they transfer pollen (fine grains) from flower to flower, so seeds are made and the next generation of plants can grow. Without them, many flowering plants would not exist.

Sow the seed

Animals help to spread seeds far and wide. Many seeds are found inside tasty fruit. After animals have eaten the fruit, these seeds are spread in their droppings.

It's fun!

Watching birds on a feeder, a hedgehog snuffling across the lawn, or newts diving in a pond is even more satisfying if you know you helped to provide and protect their homes.

Super worms

Worms make the soil healthy for growing plants. These incredible creatures eat decaying plant matter, making room for new plants. Worm poo is full of nutrients that the plants need to grow.

Your garden is a habitat

Wildlife can be big, small, or microscopic. It can live in water, soil, or in the branches of a tree. From the furriest mammal to the wriggliest bug, animals need each other. Turning your garden into a haven for wildlife means letting all animals thrive.

Food web

Here's a food web that might exist in anyone's garden. Remember, even the creatures you may not like provide food for other animals.

Too few birds could mean too many snails and caterpillars! Upsetting the balance of a wildlife garden can have disastrous effects on the plants.

Ladybirds do a good job eating aphids – a garden pest that attacks plants.

Ants, worms, and snails break down dead matter so that it enters the soil and provides nutrients, which feed plants.

Birds eat the worms that feed on rotten apples.

Green corridor
You may think a small, city garden will not make much difference to wildlife populations, but a row of neighbouring back gardens provide a large habitat. These so-called "green corridors" in cities are spied out by migrating birds and used as an area to rest as they fly across big cities.

Top predators such as a fox or owl will keep rodents in check. A variety of prey and predators keeps the food chain in balance.

Frogs will eat slugs and snails. In turn, they provide a tasty snack for a bird of prey.

Butterflies, moths, and bees live off the nectar in flowers. They become a meal for a frog or bird.

Nature SOS
It is up to us to help preserve nature, but, all too often, human beings act more like its attackers. The decline in numbers of creatures such as stag beetles, house sparrows, bees, and many types of moths and butterflies can be slowed down, and even halted, if we all do our bit.

Your Seasonal Wildlife Garden

The wildlife in your garden varies with the seasons. Spot baby animals in spring. Summer is a-buzz with wildlife. Autumn is a time of feast and plenty for wildlife. Many animals hibernate in winter.

Spring

Wake up! It's springtime. Animals such as frogs, toads, newts, hedgehogs, dormice, and spiders wake up from hibernation. Birds make nests and lay eggs, while frogs and toads release their spawn into ponds.

Summer

The warm, sunny days mean lots of food. Butterflies flit between flowers, fledgling birds take to the air, and bees work tirelessly to produce honey. Baby frogs and toads can be spotted in ponds.

Hibernation log pile

A log pile is a welcome place for animals and insects looking for somewhere to hibernate. Build this log pile in an undisturbed corner and leave it alone until spring.

1

2

3

Dig a shallow pit in a place that won't be disturbed. Pile up the logs, with the biggest logs at the bottom.

Pile up the smaller sticks on top. Fill any spaces with things such as bark, fir cones, and leaves.

Plant an ivy and trail it over the log pile. This provides even more cover for little animals.

Autumn

In autumn, a feast of berries and fruit attracts birds trying to fatten up before winter. Squirrels bury nuts for eating later. Some creatures are looking for a place to sleep out the winter.

Winter

Some animals sleep through the winter but others stay awake. This is the season when they most need our help. Birds are vulnerable and need high-energy food and water to survive the cold months ahead.

A Wildlife hedge

Hedges are alive with wildlife. They provide food and shelter, as well as a place for animals to hibernate and raise their young. Hedge flowers attract buzzing bees, butterflies, and other bugs.

Bees and butterflies
are attracted by the flowers that grow on some hedges, like privet and hawthorn.

Mice
are agile and can climb to the upper branches of hedges. They are on the lookout for snails, centipedes, and other tasty creatures.

Frogs and toads
hibernate (sleep through the winter) in old wood that gathers at the bottom of the hedge.

Grow your own hedge

If you don't have much space, you can grow a mini hedge in a long, wide container full of multi-purpose compost. Place the plants close to each other and let them knit together. Prune to manage the height. Your hedge will soon attract lots of pollinators.

Plant your hedge trees and shrubs in autumn for best results.

Voles shelter at the bottom of a hedge and use its protection to move from one part of the garden to another. These shy creatures like to stay hidden.

Birds make their nests in hedges and eat the nuts and berries of plants – or any bugs they may find there.

Insects feed and live on plants. Bugs also make a tasty snack for birds. Many are well camouflaged to blend into their green background!

Plants for a fragrant garden

A garden is not just pretty to look at — if you choose the right plants, it can surround you with sweet smells all year round. The perfume comes from oils stored in the flower's petals that are released as it opens.

Scent signals

Flowers produce strong scents to attract insects and birds to pollinate them. When flowers smell nice, animals know there is pollen and nectar inside. As they land on each bloom, pollen clings to their feet and bodies and they carry it to the next flower. But not all flowers smell sweet – some have a horrible scent to attract flies! There are some plants that only open and release their scent at night. They do this to attract night-flying pollinators, such as moths and bats.

Orchids

Orchids range in smell from fruity to spicy.

Rose

The classic rose fragrance is one of the best-loved scents. There are lots of different types of rose. They come in a range of colours, and some have petals that are particularly thick and velvety.

Honeysuckle
Honeysuckle is a strong climber that is easy to grow. The vine produces bright flowers during the summer. Plant it in the ground, then train it up a trellis.

Jasmine
This plant has delicately scented white blooms.

Freesia
A spring flower with a powerful scent.

Nicotiana
Nicotiana blooms – also known as flowering tobacco – open and release their powerful fragrance when the sun goes down. Nicotiana likes moist, fertile soil and is happiest growing in partial shade.

Lavender
Lavender is a classic scented flower. It is native to North Africa and the area around the Mediterranean Sea, but is now loved all over the world.

Starting plants for wildlife

So, you've got a patio or garden, and you want to start wildlife gardening. What should you plant? There are thousands of plants to choose from, and here's our top eight. This mixture of flowers, trees, climbers, and shrubs will make an ideal basis for your wildlife garden.

1 Wild flowers

Wildlife absolutely loves to eat wild flowers. Pick plants that grow naturally in your area.

 Sunny or partly shaded location

 Well drained, moist soil

Grows 60 cm (24 in) high

2 Clematis
(C. tangutica)

Any type of clematis is popular with wildlife, and this variety is a climber that is bushy enough for birds to nest in.

Sunny location

 Well drained soil

Grows 7 m (22 ft) high

3 Dog rose
(Rosa canina)

This climbing rose has stunning pink flowers and the branches are clothed in beautiful red rosehip fruit in autumn.

 Sunny or partly shaded location

 Well drained, moist soil

 Grows 3 m (9 ft) high

4 Long grass

Grass that has been left to grow long will do wonders for wildlife. Birds use material for nests, insects will use it as cover, and ladybirds will hibernate in long tufts.

- Sunny or partly shaded location
- Well drained soil
- Grows 1 m (39 in) high

5 Common ivy
(Hedera helix)

An evergreen climber, ivy can be grown against walls or fences, where it will provide shelter and cover for birds.

- Sunny or partly shaded location
- Well drained, moist soil
- Grows 10 m (33 ft) high

6 French lavender
(Lavandula stoechas)

Bees and butterflies love the showy, scented flowers that top this evergreen. In summer, its leaves have a scent too.

- Sunny location
- Well drained soil
- Grows 60 cm (24 in) high

7 Birch tree
(Betula pendula 'Youngii')

Young's birch has a weeping shape. It is a good choice for smaller gardens as it is fairly narrow.

- Sunny or partly shaded location
- Well drained, moist soil
- Grows 8 m (26 ft) high

8 Mixed native hedge

Native plants are ones that grow naturally in your area. This means your local animals will be used to them. Mixed native shrubs and trees provide nesting sites for birds, flowers for insects, and berries or nuts that will be eaten by many creatures.

- Sunny or partly shaded location
- Well drained, moist soil
- Grows 1–2 m (3–6 ft) high

Sunflowers

Sunflowers are great for wildlife! These plants are not only easy and fun to grow, reaching amazing heights, but they also provide year-round food for wildlife.

You will need

- Sunflower seeds
- Yoghurt pots
- Seed compost
- Polythene
- Big pot
- Garden twine
- Cane

Prevent your sunflower from toppling over by securing stems with garden twine to cane.

1 Plant seeds into yoghurt pots full of seed compost. Sow a single seed in each, 2.5 cm (1 in) deep. Water.

2 Put in a sunny place and cover with polythene. Remove the polythene when little shoots appear.

3 When your sunflower outgrows the yoghurt pot, plant it in a big container with a drainage hole in the bottom.

4 Place your plant in a sunny spot outdoors when there is no risk of frost and watch it grow.

Sunflowers provide nectar for bugs and a feast of seeds. Once it has flowered, leave the head to droop, and watch as small animals munch away at the seeds.

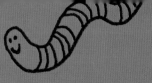

Mini nature reserve

You don't need a big garden to attract wildlife. Plant up a window box, or even an empty ice cream tub, and watch the minibeasts pay a visit!

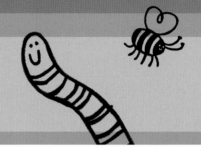

You will need

- Window box
- Broken pots
- Compost
- Trowel
- Herbs
- Trailing plants
- Gravel or bark
- Pine cone
- Saucer or jar lid

Go local! Choose plenty of plants that grow naturally in your area, as these will attract the most species of wildlife.

1 Make sure the window box has holes in the bottom. Cover the holes with broken pots.

2 Fill your window box with compost. Then plan out where you'll be positioning the plants.

3 Plant the herbs and trailing plants. Water them well.

4 Fill the top with gravel or bark to prevent water loss. Add a pine cone as a home for visiting bugs.

Include a shallow saucer of water and keep it topped up. Wildlife can use it to drink or wash.

For a year-round nature reserve, choose plants that will attract bugs throughout the seasons. Here are some suggestions:

Spring

Crocuses

Scented daffodils

Summer

Fuchsia

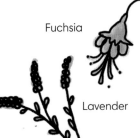

Lavender

Autumn

Chrysanthemum

Pansies

Winter

Ivy

Hardy ferns

plant a tree

Every wildlife garden should have a tree. Leafy canopies provide shelter for many creatures, while birds and small mammals build nests in their branches and eat the berries, fruit, and nuts.

1 First dig a hole. Make the hole twice as wide as the tree's "rootball", the tangled mass of roots at the bottom of the trunk.

2 Check the depth by placing a stick across the hole. It should be level with the tree's container.

3 Remove the plastic around the tree's roots and fill in the soil around the tree.

4 Ask an adult to hammer in your stake at an angle. Tie the tree to the stake.

5 Job done! Keep the tree well watered. Remove the stake when the tree is strong enough to stand on its own.

Planting a tree in a pot
is just as easy. Make sure there
is a hole in the bottom of the
pot, covered with pebbles. Place
your tree in the centre, and fill in
with loam-based compost.

Water Plants

Pond plants keep the water healthy and clear, and provide hiding places for animals. Here are some plants that thrive in ponds.

Oxygenating plants These help to stop the water turning murky.

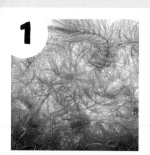

1

Hornwort
(Ceratophyllum demersum)
This bristly plant spends most of its life underwater, but the stems float to the surface during summer.

 Sunny or lightly shaded location
 Wet soil
Needs 90 cm (35 in) water depth

2

Hair grass
(Eleocharis acicularis)
This carpeting plant, which resembles grass, stays underwater all the time.

 Sunny or lightly shaded location
 Wet soil
Needs 90 cm (35 in) water depth

Deep water plants These help to keep the pond cool.

1

Water hawthorn
(Aponogeton distachyos)
This pretty plant appears above the surface from early spring to autumn.

 Sunny or partly shaded location
 Wet soil
 Needs 30-90 cm (11-35 in) water depth

2

Golden club
(Orontium aquaticum)
In spring, the golden club breaks the surface of the water with its oval leaves.

 Sunny or partly shaded location
 Wet soil
Needs 45 cm (17 in) water depth

You'll need a mix of these four types of pond plants to make a healthy pond.

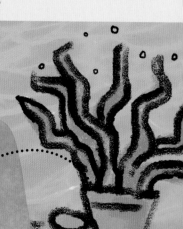

Oxygenating plants grow below the surface, giving off oxygen bubbles.

Floating plants These provide surface cover and stop the water turning green.

Frog-bit
(Hydrocharis morsus-ranae)
Frog-bit forms a mass of rounded leaves that float on the surface.

- ☀ Sunny location
- 💧 Wet soil
- 📏 Short floater

Water soldier
(Stratiotes aloides)
More suitable for a large pond, dragonflies use the plant as a perch and eat the bugs the plant attracts.

- ☀ Sunny location
- 💧 Wet soil
- 📏 Short floater

Common bladderwort
(Utricularia vulgaris)
This carnivorous plant has tiny air-filled sacs on the stems. When a bug touches the sac, it opens and water rushes in, taking the creature with it.

- ☀ Sunny location
- 💧 Wet soil
- 📏 Short floater

Marginals These provide safe havens for pond creatures.

Water forget-me-not
(Myosotis scorpiodes)
From late spring until the beginning of summer, this plant is covered in tiny blue flowers.

- ⛅ Sunny or partly shaded location
- 💧 Wet soil
- 📏 Grows 45 cm (17 in) high

Branched bur-reed
(Sparganium erectum)
This reed has narrow leaves that hide the flowering stems. The flowers become tiny seed heads in autumn.

- ⛅ Sunny or partly shaded location
- 💧 Wet soil
- 📏 Grows 100 cm (39 in) high

Dwarf reed mace
(Typha minima)
The mace's shoots grow like upright spears. The thin spike holds a brown seed head about the size of an acorn.

- ⛅ Sunny or partly shaded location
- 💧 Wet soil
- 📏 Grows 60 cm (24 in) high

Marginal plants grow in pots in the water around the pond.

Floating plants may have roots hanging free in the water.

Deep water plants are placed on or near the bottom of the pond.

Pond life

Like us, animals need to drink water and they like to bathe. Even a very small pond will quickly become alive with water bugs and other aquatic creatures.

Collect rainwater to top up the pond in hot weather.

You will need

Large plastic container

Sand

Spade

Flat stones

Gravel

Bricks or stones

Water plants

Rainwater

1

Mark out the pond's boundary by trickling sand around the edges of your plastic container.

2

Dig around the edge of the boundary first, then dig out the middle, making a hole deep enough for the container.

3

Place the container into the hole so the top is level with the ground. Fill any gaps with soil.

4

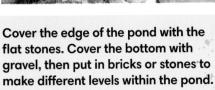

Cover the edge of the pond with the flat stones. Cover the bottom with gravel, then put in bricks or stones to make different levels within the pond.

5

Take the water plants and cover their soil with gravel to stop them floating away. Position the pots inside the pond.

6

Fill the pond with rainwater and add free-floating pond weed. Make a ramp for creatures to climb in and out by covering a piece of wood with wire mesh.

Pond dipping

Ponds are fascinating places to explore for wildlife. In this watery world you will find many unusual and bizarre-looking creatures. You can find wildlife in ponds or streams, but be careful and go with an adult as water can be hazardous.

What will you find?

Slowly sweep your net through the water. Turn the net inside-out into a container that is half-filled with water. Take a close look and see what you can identify. Below are some animals often found in ponds.

IMPORTANT:
Always return the creatures you have caught to the same part of the pond.

Tadpole, the young of frogs and toads

Mosquito larvae swim just beneath the water or hang upside down just below the surface.

Pond skaters glide effortlessly across the surface of the pond. Look out for their darting movements.

Pond snails look like their land relatives but eat pond plants and rotting plants.

Freshwater leeches are flattened, worm-like creatures that are eaten by fish and insect larvae.

Damselfly nymphs have ravenous appetites and look fearsome.

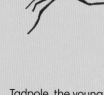

A **water beetle larva** is a fierce carnivore. Don't touch, as it ha powerful jaws and sharp fangs.

Try dipping through an area of weeds as many animals hide away in them.

Container pond

This mini pond will fit on a patio or balcony. Put it in a shady spot, and make it where you want it to be so you don't have to drag it when it's full of water.

You will need

- Clean bricks
- Gravel
- Large container
- Rainwater
- Aquatic plants
- Peg basket
- Hessian sack
- Soil
- Fish (optional)

Put a stick in your pond as an escape route for small creatures that fall in!

Fill or top up your pond with rainwater as tap water can kill fish. But if you have to use tap water, let it stand for a few days, then add your fish.

1

Arrange clean bricks and gravel in the bottom of the container. Fill two-thirds full with rainwater.

2

Put the oxygenating plants in first. Check the labels as some plants need anchoring, while others float freely in the water.

3

Stand marginal plants on the bricks at the edge of the pond. Leave these in their pots, but put a layer of gravel on the soil to keep it in place.

4

You can group marginal plants like marsh marigold and bog primula. Line a peg basket with hessian, fill with soil, plant your plants, and finish with gravel.

5

Fill the container with water, then place in one or two floating plants. Some of the water surface should be left clear of plants.

6

Now add your fish! Small goldfish or mosquito fish are perfect for mini ponds. Move fish to a larger container as they grow.

Make a frog and toad home

Frogs and toads make great garden residents. They gobble up many creatures that we consider pests, so make them feel welcome by building them a special home.

1 Dig out a hole a bit longer than the clay pot, in a cool, moist place in the shade.

2 Place the pot on its side in the hole. Bury about half of it by filling the inside with some soil.

You will need

- Trowel
- Clay pot
- Soil
- Damp leaves
- Water
- Saucer
- Gravel

3 Use some damp leaves to make a nice bed for the frog or toad inside the pot.

4 Moisten the area with a little water to keep the pot in place.

5 Place a saucer of gravel and water nearby for the frog or toad to splash about in.

Frogs and toads like a cool, damp, shallow burrow to hide away and to hibernate in over winter.

Frog Lodge

Plants for bees

Bees are the ultimate pollen and nectar collectors! Plant some of these top ten plants for bees and soon your garden will be buzzing with life.

1 Thyme
(Thymus citriodorus)
Throughout the summer, this herb is covered with tiny pink flowers that are a great favourite with bees.

- ☀ Sunny location
- 💧 Well drained soil
- 📏 Grows 30 cm (12 in) high

2 Heathers
(Calluna and Erica)
Heathers are bushes that come in many different shapes, sizes, and colours. Some flower in winter, so choose summer-flowering varieties for the bees.

- ☀ Sunny location
- 💧 Acidic, well drained soil
- 📏 Grows 30 cm (12 in) high

3 Purple sage
(Salvia officinalis 'Purpurascens')
Purple sage has pretty purple leaves that are edible. Bees love the bluish flowers that appear in summer.

- ☀ Sunny location
- 💧 Well drained, moist soil
- 📏 Grows 80 cm (31 in) high

4 Sunflowers
(Helianthus annuus)
These yellow flowers follow the sun as it moves across the sky. Bees love their luscious nectar.

- ☀ Sunny location
- 💧 Well drained, moist soil
- 📏 Grows 2.5 m (8 ft) high

5 Honeysuckle
(Lonicera varieties)
There are lots of different types of honeysuckle, ranging from white to bright red. This climber is fantastic for feeding the bees in summer.

- Sunny location
- Well drained, moist soil
- Grows 7 m (22 ft) high

6 Verbena
(Verbena bonariensis)
Verbena has a long, wiry stem with a purple pompom of flowers at the end. It flowers over a long period, from late spring to the first frosts.

- Sunny location
- Well drained, moist soil
- Grows 150 cm (59 in) high

7 Meadow cranesbill
(Geranium pratense)
Meadow cranesbill has large, saucer-shaped, purplish flowers that sit above mounds of foliage in early summer.

- Sunny or partly shaded location
- Well drained, moist soil
- Grows 60 cm (23 in) high

8 English lavender
(Lavandula angustifolia)
With its silvery, evergreen leaves and gorgeous, scented spikes of purple flowers, lavender bushes are always abuzz with nectar drinkers.

- Sunny location
- Well drained, moist soil
- Grows 1 m (39 in) high

9 Hollyhocks
(Alcea rosea)
Almost as tall as a sunflower, a hollyhock really shoots up! Its stems are studded with lots of large flowers that appear from early- to mid-summer.

- Sunny location
- Well drained soil
- Grows 1.5-2.5m (5-8 ft) high

10 Borage
(Borago officinalis)
This plant will spread quickly around the garden. It has clumps of bristly leaves and bright blue flowers all summer long.

- Sunny or partly shaded location
- Well drained soil
- Grows 60 cm (23 in) high

Create a bee hotel

Buzzing bees make the garden a lively place as they busily pollinate our favourite plants from spring to autumn. Attract bees by planting flowers and providing nesting sites.

You will need

Bamboo canes

Tape

Scissors

Modelling clay

Clay pot

1 Stand the pieces of cane on end to make a bundle. Then bind them together with tape.

2 Press the canes into a lump of modelling clay to seal off one end.

Some solitary bees seek out hollow plant stems, or holes and cracks in bricks or wood to nest in. As an alternative bee hotel, ask an adult to drill 15 cm (6 in) deep holes, 6–10 mm (¼ in) wide, into a piece of untreated wood.

3 Put the canes into the pot, open ends facing out. Use more clay to wedge the bundle tightly inside the pot.

4 Leave the pot on its side in a sunny, dry spot for solitary bees to find.

Fossils show that bees first appeared on earth 150 million years ago.

What bee did I see?

There are about 40,000 species of bee in the world. There are only seven species that make honey, which makes them very special. These bees live together in hives, but over 90% of bees are solitary and like to live alone.

Honey bee

Bumble bee

Mining bee

Ladybird Sanctuary

Ladybirds are a gardener's best friend. Although tiny, these spotted creatures have a ravenous appetite for aphids and other tiny pests that cause damage to plants.

You will need

- Plastic bottle
- Scissors
- Corrugated cardboard
- Twigs

1 Ask an adult to cut the top off a plastic bottle and cut out a piece of corrugated cardboard about the length of the bottle.

2 Roll the cardboard up tightly. Place the rolled up cardboard into the plastic bottle.

3 Fill the hole with twigs for the ladybirds to land on. Place the bottle in a dry, sheltered spot.

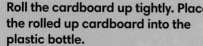

4 The bottom of the bottle needs to be higher than the opening to allow water to drain away.

A single ladybird can eat up to 5,000 aphids in its lifetime.

The spottiest ladybirds have 24 spots on their back.

Hibernation

Ladybirds often use the same site to hibernate (sleep through the winter) every year and sometimes hibernate in colonies of hundreds of ladybirds. It is thought they release a scent to attract others, as huddling together helps them keep warm.

Plants for caterpillars and butterflies

Caterpillars are fussy eaters so butterflies only lay their eggs on plants that their hungry offspring will eat. Once they transform into butterflies, they often seek out plants with nectar-filled flowers.

Plants for caterpillars

1 Nettles
(Urtica dioica)
A patch of nettles is the favourite plant of red admiral, peacock, and small tortoiseshell butterflies.

- Sunny or lightly shaded location
- Moist soil
- Grows 1.5 m (5 ft) high

2 Bird's foot trefoil
(Lotus corniculatus)
This pretty yellow wildflower with red tips is loved by the caterpillars of many types of butterfly.

- Sunny location
- Well drained soil
- Grows 30 cm (11 in) high

3 Nasturtium
(Tropaeolum)
The caterpillars of the small and large cabbage white butterflies love to munch on nasturtiums.

- Sunny location
- Well drained soil
- Grows 30 cm–3 m (11 in–10 ft) high

4 Garlic mustard
(Alliaria petiolata)
Green-veined white butterflies and orange-tip butterflies lay eggs on this plant. Its leaves smell of garlic.

- Sunny or partly shaded location
- Wet soil
- Grows 1 m (39 in) high

Plants for butterflies

1 French marigold
(Tagetes patula)
This small, pretty flower is found in yellow, orange, and red. The varieties with simple, single flowers are best for butterflies.

- ☀ Sunny location
- 💧 Well drained soil
- 📏 Grows 30 cm (11 in) high

2 Helen's flower
(Helenium)
These flowers bloom from late summer until early autumn when daisies grow over it. It spreads slowly but eventually forms into a pretty, flowery clump.

- ☀ Sunny location
- 💧 Moist soil
- 📏 Grows 90 cm (3 ft) high

3 Ice plant
(Sedum spectabile)
The tiny, bright pink flowers that perch on top of the stems of this plant are delicious to both bees and butterflies.

- ☀ Sunny location
- 💧 Well drained soil
- 📏 Grows 45 cm (18 in) high

4 Michaelmas daisy
(Aster novae-belgii)
This is more like a bush than a flower. The bush gets covered with daisy-like flowers from late summer to autumn.

- ⛅ Sunny or partly shaded location
- 💧 Moist soil
- 📏 Grows 60 cm–1.5 m (23 in–5 ft) high

5 Bugbane
(Cimicifuga simplex)
Bugbane is a great nectar provider, especially in autumn when butterflies are running out of summer flowers.

- ⛅ Sunny or partly shaded location
- 💧 Moist soil
- 📏 Grows 1.2 m (4 ft) high

6 Hyssop
(Hyssopus officinalis)
This evergreen herb has blueish flowers that last throughout summer and into early autumn, providing a summer feast for butterflies.

- ☀ Sunny location
- 💧 Well drained soil
- 📏 Grows 60 cm (23 in) high

Butterfly feeder

Beautiful butterflies love to eat sweet things, like the nectar from flowers, or very ripe fruit. You can make them a delicious dinner using just an overripe banana.

You will need

- Very ripe banana
- Knife
- Pen or pencil
- Card
- Scissors
- Stickers
- Glue
- Lollipop sticks

If you have a whole bunch of overripe bananas, use the rest to bake some banana bread.

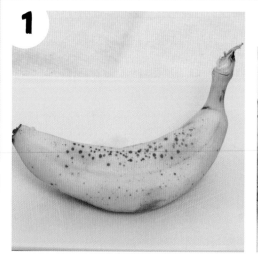

1 Leave a banana in the fruit bowl for a week, until it gets brown spots. Mash it with your hands until the inside is all squishy.

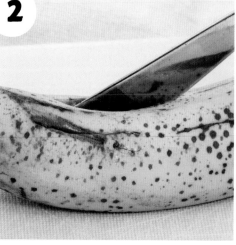

2 Use a table knife to carefully cut holes in the top and sides of the banana. This is how the butterflies will get at the squishy fruit.

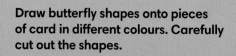

3 Draw butterfly shapes onto pieces of card in different colours. Carefully cut out the shapes.

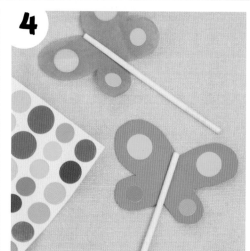

4 Stick circular stickers onto your shapes to make paper butterflies. Glue them onto lollipop sticks, then use them to decorate your banana.

A butterfly tastes through its feet! When it lands on the banana, it will taste it first then use its long mouth to feed.

Butterfly spotter
Keep an eye out for different types of butterflies that might visit your feeder. How many can you spot?

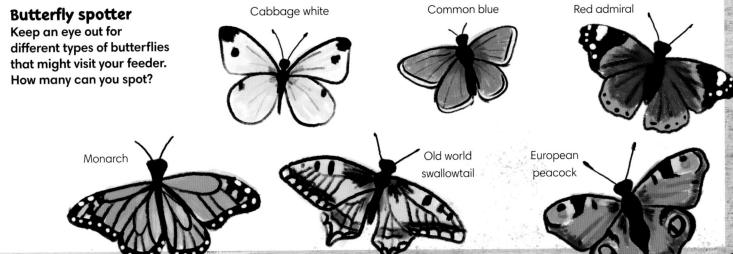

Cabbage white

Common blue

Red admiral

Monarch

Old world swallowtail

European peacock

Pet's Corner

Why not grow some tasty treats for your pets? Cats, dogs, guinea pigs, and rabbits love to nibble plants, but it's important to provide them with ones they can safely eat.

You will need

- Plastic bottle
- Scissors
- Marker pen
- Water bowl
- Gravel
- Compost
- Water
- Pet-friendly seeds

Grow in a sunny place and use well-drained soil. Grass seeds germinate within 1-2 weeks and the grasses are ready to be nibbled after 4 weeks.

Sow barley, oats, and wheat for your rabbit. Sow Timothy meadow grass and plantains for your guinea pigs.

1

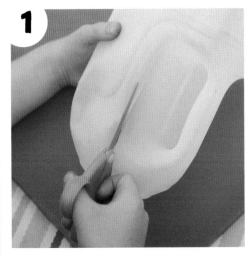

For the labels, cut a panel from a plastic bottle and then draw an outline of the shape of your pet with a marker pen.

2

Add features, such as whiskers, using the marker. Then cut out around the pet shape.

3

Ask an adult to drill holes in the base of the bowl. Fill with a little gravel, add compost, and water.

4

If the seeds are large, such as cat grass for cats, cover them with soil using your fingertips.

5

If the seeds are small, such as Lucerne grass for your dog, sprinkle them over the surface of the moist compost and add a thin layer of soil on top.

6

Keep the containers well watered as the plants grow. Trim the plants using scissors to keep them at a good height for your pet.

Recycled garden

Re-using and recycling in the garden is a great way
to reduce your waste and live a greener life.

Why Recycle in the garden?

Recycling is when you turn an old object or material into something new. You can sort your waste and send it to a recycling plant. You can also re-use objects that are old or broken by finding new uses for them at home.

Why should I recycle?

Reduce pollution
Re-using objects instead of buying them new saves energy and the resources that are used to make them. For example, making things from plastic uses up oil, which is a fossil fuel that takes millions of years to form underground.

As good as new
Plants and animals don't care if things are broken! Plants are just as happy to grow in cracked containers as new ones.

Save habitats
Recycling and re-using helps the environment beyond your garden. Insects, birds, and mammals all need places to live and have their young. If we create more landfills to throw rubbish into, more animal habitats will be destroyed.

How can I avoid waste in the garden?

Collect water to use on plants

A rainwater butt is a barrel you leave out in the garden to collect rainwater. This can be used to water plants or fill ponds. It's better for plants and animals than tapwater because it hasn't been treated with any chemicals.

Don't buy it, recycle it

You can save money and the environment by re-using cans, bottles, pots, and tubs from around the home as containers. Just make sure there are holes in the bottom for water to drain out.

Composting

Food waste from the kitchen, and grass cuttings and dead leaves from the garden, can be used to make compost. Not only does this save green waste from being sent to landfills, it's a great, free way to add nutrients to the soil.

Recycle and renew

What can you do with all your fruit and vegetable peelings, old plants, grass cuttings, and autumn leaves? You can use them to make wonderful, rich soil or layers of mulch for the plants you'll grow next year.

Making your own compost

If you want to make compost but you only have a small space, you can buy a plastic compost bin. Add layers of waste that will rot down inside the bin and you'll have excellent, crumbly compost six to nine months later.

1 Choose a partly sunny site for the compost bin. Place the bin on earth and not concrete, so that water can drain out and helpful bugs can get in.

2 Keep filling your bin with equal amounts of "green" and "brown" waste to get the best mix.

3 Cover the bin with a lid, or an old doormat to keep in the heat to encourage the bugs. Sprinkle in some soil and, every month or so, ask an adult to help you mix the top few layers with a fork, so the waste will rot faster. You'll notice your heap rotting down and reducing in size. It will smell earthy!

The **greens** are the young, wet waste, such as vegetable peelings, grass cuttings, and teabags, that will rot quickly. The provide nitrogen and moisture.

The **browns** are the tough, dry waste, such as scrunche paper, egg boxes, fallen lea and your pet's bedding. The provide fibre and carbon ar form air pockets for the bug

Through composting, the goodness from decaying plants can be recycled and turned into rich soil for new plants to use.

Don't put these in your bin: cat litter, dog poo, disposable nappies, glossy magazines and newspapers, cooked food, oil, meat or fish.

Compost critters

Rich, crumbly compost is partly made up of bugs' very dark poo. So you'll see many busy bugs living in your bin. Some bugs feed on the green and brown organic waste you've put in. Others shred this waste and tunnel through it, mixing it up.

Smaller, organic waste-eating bugs attract bigger bugs to the compost heap, searching for food.

We all eat organic waste.

Millipede

Pill millipede

Garden snail

Slug

Earthworm

Compost mites

If you have these, you'll get these!

Look out! We eat smaller bugs.

Earwig

Rove beetle

Ant

Spider

Ground beetle

Centipede

The magic of mulching

Another great gardening tip is to try mulching. Mulch is a layer covering the surface of the soil that provides nutrients to the plants, keeps in the moisture, prevents weeds growing, and helps to protect the roots from cold. Try tree bark, pine needles, grass clippings, and even seaweed. Recycled glass, beads, or seashells can be used as decorative mulch.

Make your own lovely leaf mould

Punch a few holes in the side and bottom of a bin liner. Gather up piles of autumn leaves and put them in the bag. When the bag is almost full, sprinkle the leaves with water, then shake the bag and tie it up. Store it in a shady spot. After a year, the leaves will have rotted down into a rich, crumbly mixture. Spread this over your soil, and your plants will thrive.

Collecting seeds

Many of the plants you have grown have produced seeds, which you could collect and then use to grow new plants next year.

You will need

Healthy plant

Scissors

Paper bag

 The secret of success is to collect the seeds at the right time. Choose a dry, windless day to collect your seeds so they don't get damp or blow away.

1

Choose a healthy plant. When seed heads or seedpods have ripened, cut off the entire seed head or pod.

2

Remove the seeds using your fingers. Leave the seeds to dry in a warm place. Store the seeds in a dry, cool place until spring.

3

Some seeds that are very dry may need soaking before planting to encourage them to germinate.

4

Why not trade seeds with other gardeners and give some to your friends to have a go, too?

Angelica seeds

Pepper seeds

Bean seeds

Sunflower seeds can be collected when they look big and brown. Pinch them out into a paper bag.

Eggshell planters

If you've eaten eggs, you can put the leftover shells to good use by planting seeds in them. The shells protect your delicate seeds and even deter small creatures like slugs that would like to eat your seedlings.

1

Wash and dry leftover eggshells and put them back in the egg box they came in.

2

Fill the eggshells with soil, making sure it is not too packed in. Sow one seed in each eggshell.

You will need

Clean eggshells

Egg box

Quick-growing seeds, such as nasturtium

3

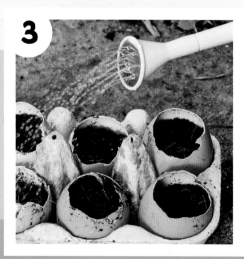

Water the eggshells and put them in a warm, sunny place. Either a windowsill or a bright corner of your garden would be good.

4

Give the plants a little water every day until seedlings sprout. This should only take a week. If no seedlings sprout, trying moving the tray somewhere warmer.

5

Once you have healthy seedlings, take them out of the box and plant them in the soil. They'll eventually need taking out of the eggshells so their roots can grow.

Try crumbling up eggshell and sprinkling it around your plants to provide nutrients.

Stunning Succulents

Succulents make gorgeous indoor plants, and they are easy to take care of. Once you have a succulent, you can create more of them by "propagating". This means growing a new plant from a part of the old one.

You will need

- Succulent plant
- Paper
- Tray
- Soil
- Spray bottle

1 Buy a healthy-looking succulent plant from the garden centre. Pick one in a colour you like, because you're growing more just like it!

2 Gently twist and remove around 12 leaves – be careful not to tear them. Space them out on some paper, and leave them to dry for a few days.

3 Fill a tray with soil. Once the leaves look and feel dry, arrange them in a circular shape in the tray.

4 Spritz your circle with water, then keep spritzing them every day. After a week, you'll notice some tiny roots start to sprout from the ends of your leaves.

5 Eventually new, tiny succulents will start to sprout where the roots are. If you take care of them, they will grow into full-size succulents!

Try growing a few different-coloured succulents and create a gorgeous rainbow garden.

Cork planters

You can find corks either stopping up bottles or being sold in craft stores. Using them to create mini planters is a great way to re-use them. Once you've grown some tiny succulents using the steps on pages 104-105, you can plant them in your corks.

You will need

- Table knife
- Corks
- Craft glue
- Magnet
- Soil
- Tiny succulent
- Fridge

1

Using an ordinary table knife, carefully scrape a hole in the top of a cork. Ask for help from an adult if you're not confident in doing this.

2

Put a blob of craft glue on the back of a small magnet. Hold the magnet onto the side of the cork until the glue dries and the magnet sticks.

3

Fill the hole in the top of your cork with soil. Do not water as it will make the cork soggy.

4

Plant a tiny succulent or other mini plant into the soil. Then make a few more cork planters!

If your cork is too heavy and swings around on the magnetic surface, try gluing a second magnet above it.

Creative containers

Unusual pots for your plants will make your gardening projects extra interesting. Any container that has sides can be used, so keep a look out for possible ones to recycle, or make your own from a comic book or newspaper.

You will need

- Newspaper or comic book page
- Drinking glass
- Soil
- Seeds

Keep your seedlings inside somewhere warm and bright during the winter months. Plant them outside in spring.

1 Take a page from a newspaper or comic. Fold over one long edge, twice, to make the top of your container.

2 Roll the paper around a glass. Push the unfolded edge into the glass to make the base of your paper pot.

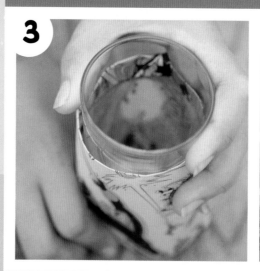

3 Slide the paper off the glass. You can use the glass to help you flatten out the base of your pot against a table.

4 Fill the pot with soil and then it is ready for sowing the seeds. Once the weather is warm outside, the seedlings can be planted in their pots straight into the soil. The paper will disintegrate over time.

Almost anything can become a planter. Before you throw away an old or broken object, consider making it a home for a plant.

Pot labels and markers

When you plant seeds, remember to make a label. When seedlings appear, it can be get hard to tell which plant is which. Your labels can be as simple as lollipop sticks with names written on them, or you can have some fun making and decorating more elaborate labels.

Tall labels

Labels on sticks will stand out in a pot. They are ideal for bushy plants, such as lamb's lettuce or herbs. Waterproof labels can be made using pizza bases or the bottom of a plastic bottle.

Wildlife labels

Make a note of which plants are good at attracting wildlife – check the back of the seed packet for information. Waterproof labels can be made using washed pizza bases.

Use a permanent marker to make it waterproof.

Stone markers

Mark around where you've planted seeds with colourful stones. What eye-catching designs will you paint? Why not paint some animal markers or the first letter of your name?

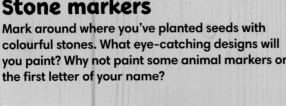

Paint me!

Funny markers

Plant funny ping-pong labels all over your garden. Simply make a hole in a ping-pong ball and stick it on top of a plant cane. Use waterproof pens and paint to decorate.

Lolly stick labels

Lolly sticks are very handy as labels for small seed pots. Use pens to draw a picture of the vegetable you have planted or to make a pattern.

Paint the end of a lolly stick to measure how deep to make your seed hole.

1 cm
(0.3 in)

2 cm
(0.8 in)

3 cm
(1.25 in)

basil

Mini greenhouses

Big greenhouses are used in gardens to grow fruit and vegetables that need warm temperatures to thrive. You can make mini versions for your windowsill to house some spiky cacti – they love a warm, dry place to grow.

You will need

Glass jar

Tape

Glass pen

Soil

Trowel

Paper

Cactus

Gravel

Water your cactus every two weeks between spring and autumn. Do not water in the winter.

1 Place a piece of tape on a clean, dry jar. Using a special pen for drawing on glass, use the tape as a guide to draw patterns all over the jar.

2 When you're happy with your patterns, put some soil into the jar to create a habitat for your plant.

3 Carefully lower your cactus into the jar. Put a funnel made from paper around your cactus to stop soil from getting caught in its spines. Cover the roots with soil.

4 Remove the paper funnel. Cover the top of the soil with gravel. This looks good and helps the cactus grow. Now make more and create a greenhouse garden!

Strawberry boots

Did you know that you can grow delicious strawberries in your back garden? Planting them in a pot is fine, but it's much more fun to recycle old Wellington boots!

1

Ask an adult to cut a hole in the side of the boot. Make sure it's big enough to fit your plant's roots into.

2

Put a little gravel in the boots to allow for drainage. Add enough soil to come up to the hole in the side.

You will need

- Wellington boots
- Scissors or scalpel
- Gravel
- Soil
- Strawberry plants

3

Push a strawberry plant sideways into the hole, then fill the boot with more soil, almost up to the top.

4

Place another plant into the top of the boot. Level off the soil and press down firmly. Repeat this with the other boot. Water both boots well.

5

Place your boots in a sunny spot and keep them well watered. The plants should make strawberries within 12 weeks.

Rub petroleum jelly over the sides of the boots to keep slugs and snails away.

Bird bathroom

Many gardeners put food out for birds, but few remember to give them water. A birdbath and shower will give them somewhere to drink and to wash, keeping them healthy and happy.

You will need

- Shallow bowl
- Clean pebbles
- Decorations
- Plastic bottle with cap
- Drawing pin
- Water
- String

Where to put it

Birds will only visit your birdbath if they feel safe from predators. Place it close to bushes, where they can fly to if they become alarmed. Avoid placing it by ground-covering shrubs where cats could be hiding.

1

Cover the bottom of a shallow bowl with a layer of pebbles. Place the bowl on a small sturdy table or a level tree stump.

2

Add a small decoration such as a pebble sculpture, a flagpole, or a plastic frog to your birdbath.

3

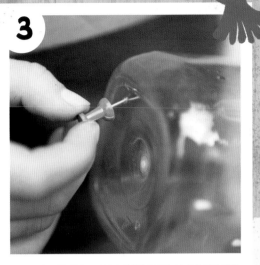

Make a tiny hole in the bottom of the bottle, using the tip of a drawing pin. Decorate the bottle if you wish.

4

Add water to the bottle and screw on the bottle cap. The water will flow in a stream at first, then slow to a steady drip.

5

Attach the string to the bottle. Hang it above the bowl so that the water drips into it. The rippling effect will attract the birds.

6

Add some water to the bowl. Every few weeks, clean the bowl with soapy water to remove droppings and bacteria.

Bird feeder

Watching garden birds is great fun and they are easy to attract to your garden.
All you need to do is hang up a feeder and fill it with the food that birds love to eat.

1

Cut a hole in the side of the clean carton about 5 cm (2 in) from the bottom to make a doorway. Ask an adult if you find this tricky.

2

Cut out brown and green leaf shapes from plastic bags and stick them on the carton with the glue.

3

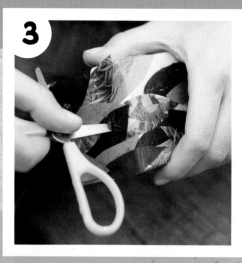

Poke several small holes in the bottom of the carton with scissors so that rainwater can drain out.

4

Staple the top closed. Pierce a hole in the top and thread the wire through to hang up the feeder.

5

Poke a twig through the carton just below the doorway for a perch. Add bird seed and hang the feeder.

There are about 10,000 different species of birds in the world.

House sparrows are the most widely spread wild bird around the world, but their numbers have declined dramatically in recent years.

House sparrow

Rufous-winged sparrow

Owl nesting boot

Owls mainly come out after dark. If you're lucky you might spot one of these amazing birds. Give them somewhere to nest and listen out for their distinctive hooting call.

You will need

Adult-sized Wellington boot

Skewer

Wood shavings or sawdust

Wire

Stepladder

1 Poke holes in the bottom of the boot with a skewer so that rainwater can drain out. Get an adult to help you with this in case the skewer slips.

2 Drop two handfuls of wood shavings or sawdust into the boot as bedding for eggs and owlets (baby owls).

Many natural nesting sites are under threat. This treetop refuge will give small species of owls somewhere safe and warm to raise their young.

3 Secure the boot in place by wrapping wire around the branch and boot. Use a stepladder to reach up to a high branch.

4 Look out for signs of use such as white droppings. After the owls have left, clean out the boot and add more sawdust ready for the next family of owls.

Bird experts think there are 217 different species of owl in the world, including snowy, tawny, and barn owls.

Self-watering Seedlings

Plastic bottles make excellent planters for growing seeds into seedlings. These clever planters mean they can drink as much water as they want. They are also a good way to re-use plastic water bottles so they don't end up in the rubbish dump.

You will need

Plastic bottle

Pencil

Scissors

String

Water

Soil

1

Using a pencil, poke a hole into the soft plastic top of a clean drinks bottle.

2

Cut the bottle into two parts. Cut about two thirds of the way up the bottle so that the top part is shorter. The edges are sharp so consider asking an adult to help.

3

Using the pencil, poke a length of string through the hole in the bottle top. This will allow the plant to drink.

4

Fill the bottom of the bottle with water. Put the top of the bottle into the bottom, with the cap facing down and the string dangling into the water.

5

Fill the top of the bottle with soil. Plant one or two seeds of your choice and put them in a sunny spot to grow. No need to water!

Try poking a few holes into the cap of a plastic milk bottle and using it as a watering can.

Glossary

Aphids
Tiny, green insects that eat sap and can cause a lot of damage to plants. Ladybirds eat aphids.

Bud
A tiny part on a plant's twig or stem that grows into a leaf.

Bulb
A round, underground part of a plant that can be planted to grow into a full plant. Bulbs include onions and many spring flowers.

Cactus
A spiny plant that can store water inside its stem.

Cane
Usually made of bamboo, canes are stiff rods that can be used to support plants as they grow.

Carbon dioxide
A gas that plants need to make food through the process of photosynthesis.

Carnivorous plant
A plant that captures and eats insects.

Compost
A rich mixture of decayed plants that is added to the soil.

Crop
The harvest of fruit or vegetables that you get from a particular plant.

Earthing up
Building up soil around a potato plant's stem to encourage it to send outroots where new potatoes will grow.

Eco-friendly
Any activity that considers the impact on the environment and tries to help rather than harm.

Ericaceous soil
Acidic soil suitable for growing plants such as blueberries.

Fertilizer
A mixture that encourages plants to grow.

Flower
The part of a plant where the male and female parts are found. Flowers usually have bright, colourful petals to attract insects.

Fruit
The part of a plant that forms when a flower is pollinated. The fleshy part protects the seeds inside.

Germination
When seeds sprout and start to grow.

Habitat
The place where an animal lives. Different animals prefer different types of habitat, for example frogs enjoy ponds.

Hibernation
Sleeping through the winter months to save energy.

Marginal plants
Plants that can grow with their roots in the water at the edge of a pond.

Microscopic
Smaller than you can see with your eyes.

Mould
Another word for fungus. Some moulds attack plants. They can easily grow in waterlogged soil.

Mulch
A thick layer covering the surface of the soil that keeps in moisture, prevents weeds from growing, and helps to protect the roots from cold. Some mulches also add nutrients to the soil.

Nectar
Sweet liquid that flowers use to attract bees and butterflies.

Nutrients
Substances that help a plant or animal to grow.

Ovary
One of the female parts of a flower. Ovaries contain tiny ovules, which grow into seeds.

Oxygenation
Putting oxygen into water or the air.

Photosynthesis
The process by which plants make their food, using carbon dioxide gas and sunlight.

Pest
Any bug or animal in the garden that harms plants.

Pollen
Tiny grains that are carried from flower to flower by pollinators.

Pollination
The process where pollen is carried from one flower to another, so that it can grow seeds.

Pollinator
Any insect or animal that carries pollen from one flower to another. Pollinators include bees and bats.

Pollution
Dirty and harmful substances that damage the environment.

Propagation
Growing new plants from parts of a plant, such as the leaves.

Pruning
Cutting back some parts of a plant to help the whole thing grow.

Recycling
Using materials again instead of throwing them away.

Ripening
When fruit grows to its full size and becomes ready to eat.

Rootball
The tangled mass of roots at the bottom of a tree.

Seed
A part of a flowering plant that contains a baby plant and a store of food to get it started.

Seedling
A young plant that has just started to grow.

Sprout
A spiny plant that can store water inside its stem.

Stamen
The male part of a plant, where pollen is stored.

Stigma
One of the female parts of a plant. This is where pollen from other flowers is gathered so the plant can make seeds.

Style
Connects the stigma to the ovary in a flower.

Succulent
A type of cactus which has fleshy leaves and comes in many colours.

Transplant
To move a young plant that has outgrown its pot into a larger container.

Vegetable
The edible leaf, stem, or root of a plant. Some plants that are called vegetables, such as peppers and tomatoes, are actually fruits.

Index

Acknowledgements

DK would like to thank: Clare Lloyd , Hélène Hilton, Becky Walsh, and Abigail Luscombe for editorial help; Helen Peters for the index.

The publisher would like to thank the following for their kind permission to reproduce their photographs:

(Key: a-above; b-below/bottom; c-centre; f-far; l-left; r-right; t-top)

1 Dreamstime.com: Bidouze Stéphane / Smithore (b).
4 123RF.com: Iryna Denysova (bl). Dreamstime.com: Marilyn Barbone (cr). 10 Alamy Stock Photo: AidanStock (br); Alexander Vinokurov (ca); Metta focus (cra); Metta foto (cl); Sergey Skleznev (cb); Kevin Wheal (bc). 12 Getty Images: Will Heap (tl). 16 Dreamstime.com: Stocksolutions (br). 18 Dreamstime.com: Stocksolutions (cl). 20 Dreamstime.com: Stocksolutions (cl). 22 Dreamstime.com: Stocksolutions (cl). 24 Dreamstime.com: Stocksolutions (cr). 26 Dreamstime.com: Slogger; Stocksolutions (br). 28 Dreamstime.com: Stocksolutions (cr). 29 123RF.com: Nataliia Melnychuk (b). 30 Dreamstime.com: Stocksolutions (cl). 32 123RF.com: Nataliia Melnychuk. Dreamstime.com: Stocksolutions (crb). 34 Dreamstime.com: Stocksolutions (cr). 36 Dreamstime.com: Stocksolutions (cl). 38 Dreamstime.com: Stocksolutions (cr). 40 Dreamstime.com: Stocksolutions (cr). 42 Dreamstime.com: Stocksolutions (cr). 43 123RF.com: Songsak Paname. 44 Dreamstime.com: Stocksolutions (cla). 46 Dreamstime.com: Stocksolutions (cl). 47 Dorling Kindersley: Alan Buckingham (tr). Dreamstime.com: Richard Gunion / Shootalot (tc). GAP Photos: (b). 48 Dreamstime.com: Stocksolutions (cr). 50 Dreamstime.com: Luis2007 (c/Background); Stocksolutions (cl). 51 123RF.com: Weerachai Khumfu (tl). Alamy Stock Photo: Martin Shields (b). Dreamstime.com: Christian Jung (tc); Lestertairpolling (tr). 52 123RF.com: Papan Saenkutrueang (bl). Dreamstime.com: Shih-hao Liao / Photoncatcher (cl). 53 123RF.com: Blend Images (bl). 54-55 Dreamstime.com: Adistock (Background). 54 Dreamstime.com: Thai Noipho (cr); Svetlana Larina / Blair witch (clb, cb). 55 123RF.com: 5second (b); Timothy Holle (cl); Denis Tabler (c); Marie-Ann Daloia / mariedaloia (c/Squirrel); Eric Isselee (tr). Dreamstime.com: Shih-hao Liao / Photoncatcher (cr); Tomert (c/Photo frames). 57 Dreamstime.com: Stephen Griffith (tr). 58 Dreamstime.com: Artjazz (cr); Prentiss40 (cl). 59 Dorling Kindersley: Oxford Scientific Films (cr). Dreamstime.com: Volodymyr Kucherenko (cl). 60 Dorling Kindersley: Liberty's Owl, Raptor and Reptile Centre, Hampshire, UK (bc). 60-61 123RF.com: Jürgen Fälchle (c). 61 123RF.com: William Rodrigues Dos Santos (br). Dreamstime.com: Mikelane45 (bc); Susan Robinson / Suerob (bl). 62 123RF.com: Igor Terekhov (bc); udra (bl). Dreamstime.com: Whiskybottle (br). 63 123RF.com: annete (br). Dreamstime.com: Phanuwatn (bl); Alfio Scisetti (cla). 64 Dreamstime.com: Andrew Oxley (clb). 65 Depositphotos Inc: Arrxxx (cla). Dreamstime.com: Jochenschneider (tl); Mysikrysa (bl). iStockphoto.com: Martin

Wahlborg (clb). 66 Dreamstime.com: Stocksolutions (cla). 67 123RF.com: Robert D Hale (b). Dorling Kindersley: Peter Anderson / RHS Hampton Court Flower Show 2014 (tl). Dreamstime.com: Alfio Scisetti / Scisettialfio (tc). 68 Dreamstime.com: Stocksolutions (cl). 69 Dreamstime.com: Adistock (Background). 70 Dreamstime.com: Stocksolutions (cr). 71 Alamy Stock Photo: Avalon / Photoshot License. 72 123RF.com: PaylessImages (cb). Dreamstime.com: Kewuwu (ca); Verastuchelova (cla). 72-73 Dreamstime.com: trekandshoot (b). 73 123RF.com: maxaltamor (ca/Sparganium erectum). Alamy Stock Photo: Frank Hecker (cb); M & J Bloomfield (clb). Dreamstime.com: Argenlant (ca); Toni Genes (cla). 74 Dreamstime.com: Stocksolutions (br). 75 Dreamstime.com: Luis2007 (Background). 76 Dreamstime.com: Stocksolutions (cl). 78 Dreamstime.com: Stocksolutions (cr). 80 Dreamstime.com: John Pavel (c). 81 123RF.com: Thanongsak Onhatpho (clb). Dorling Kindersley: RHS Hampton Court Flower Show 2012 (fcla); Mark Winwood / RHS Wisley (tl). Dreamstime.com: Michael Smith (cl). 82 Dreamstime.com: Luis2007 (Background); Stocksolutions (cl). 83 Dorling Kindersley: Neil Fletcher (br). 84 Dreamstime.com: Stocksolutions (cla). 85 Dreamstime.com: Kellie Eldridge (br). 86 123RF.com: Simona Pavan (bl). Dreamstime.com: Tt (cl). 88 Dreamstime.com: Stocksolutions (cl). 90 Dreamstime.com: Stocksolutions (cl). 92 Dreamstime.com: Stocksolutions (cl). 94 123RF.com: Phanuwat Nandee (tr). 95 123RF.com: windsurfer62 (br). 98 Dreamstime.com: Stocksolutions (cla). 99 Dreamstime.com: Rrodrickbeiler (tc). 100 Dreamstime.com: Stocksolutions (cr). 102 Dreamstime.com: Stocksolutions (cla). 103 Dreamstime.com: Harrydo (b); Taniawild (tc). 104 Dreamstime.com: Stocksolutions (cl). 106 Dreamstime.com: Stocksolutions (cla). 108 Dreamstime.com: Adistock (Background). 108-109 Dreamstime.com: Bidouze Stéphane / Smithore (b). 109 Dreamstime.com: Adistock (Background). 110 Dreamstime.com: Stocksolutions (cl). 112 Dreamstime.com: Luis2007 (Background); Stocksolutions (cr). 113 Dorling Kindersley: Alan Buckingham (br). 114 Dreamstime.com: Stocksolutions (cr). 116 Dreamstime.com: Stocksolutions (cl). 118 Dreamstime.com: Stocksolutions (cr). 118-119 Dreamstime.com: Luis2007 (Background). 119 123RF.com: Callum Redgrave-Close (br). Dorling Kindersley: Alan Murphy (bc). Dreamstime.com: Paul Reeves / Paulreevesphotography (bl). 120 Dreamstime.com: Stocksolutions (cl). 121 Dreamstime.com: Assoonas (br); Ondřej Prosický (t, bl). 122 Dreamstime.com: Stocksolutions (br). 123 Dreamstime.com: Luis2007 (Background)

Cover images: Front: Dreamstime.com: Luis2007 c; Back: Dreamstime.com: Artjazz clb, Luis2007 c, Sahua bc; Spine: Dreamstime.com: Luis2007 c

All other images © Dorling Kindersley
For further information see: www.dkimages.com